Map Crosswords

25 Map/Crossword Puzzles That Teach Map and Geography Skills

by Spencer Finch

SCHOLASTIC
PROFESSIONAL BOOKS

NEW YORK • TORONTO • LONDON • AUCKLAND • SYDNEY

Cover design by Vincent Ceci and Jaime Lucero
Interior design and maps by Solutions by Design

ISBN 0-590-89646-6

12 11 10 9 8   1 2/0

Printed in the U.S.A.

Table of Contents

Introduction

Perhaps no part of the social studies curriculum has so many applications outside the classroom as using maps. On a daily basis, we use maps to find our way in the world: from getting off the right highway exit to understanding the latest trends in culture, politics, and demography.

The maps in this book represent a wide range of map skills and cartographic styles. The intent is to expose students to a variety of maps so that they can develop skills to apply to the maps they encounter in the real world or in other content areas. Some map skills, such as understanding longitude and latitude, are notoriously difficult for students to grasp, and these might require additional explanation or practice. Other maps, such as product maps, are fairly straightforward, and most students will be able to proceed on their own in working out the puzzles for these. The maps in this book are organized roughly in ascending order of difficulty.

Maps are also fun! They offer creative ways to present all sorts of information in a visual format. They can be used as a springboard for discussions about geography, history, economics, and current events. Many of these puzzles are well suited to serve as extension activities for other studies. For example, the Montana Products map could easily complement the study of U.S. geography or national economics. We hope that your students will find the maps fun and engaging and the crossword puzzles challenging and thought-provoking.

Highways

Arizona

Highway maps are one of the most popular kinds of maps around. People use them everyday, when they are driving on vacation, or just finding their way around a new place. Highway maps don't just show where roads lead to. They also show the different types of roads: big interstate highways as well as small and winding state highways.

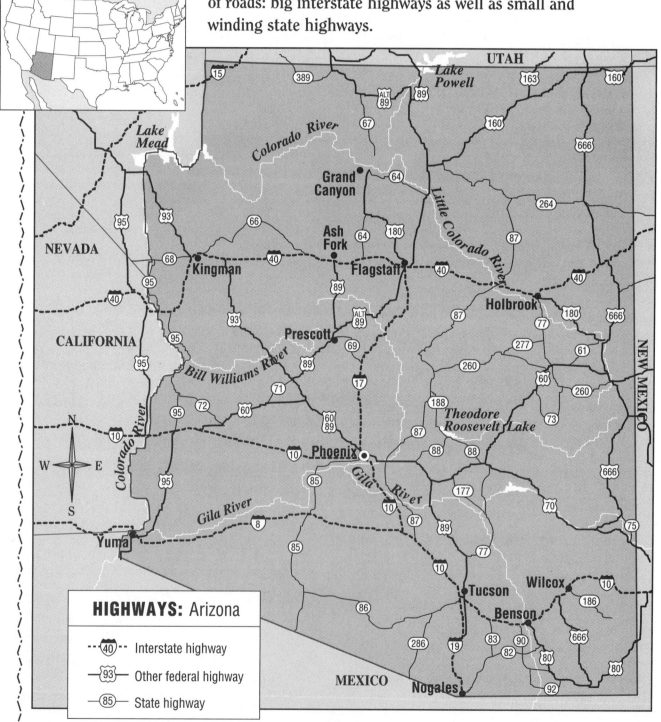

HIGHWAYS: Arizona

- - (40) - - Interstate highway
- —(93)— Other federal highway
- —(85)— State highway

Highways

Across

1 Routes 77, 180, and 40 all come together in which town?

4 Going north on Route 666 will land you in which state?

5 On highways you can drive _____ than on small roads.

6 If you were arriving in Arizona from California on Route 40, the first town you would hit would be _____.

11 The big highways of Route 17 and 10 meet in which city?

12 The smaller roads on this map are _____ highways.

15 If you follow Route 180 north from Flagstaff, where will you end up?

18 You can get to _____ by traveling southeast on Route 89 from Phoenix.

20 Any highway that goes east will take you to this state.

22 Route 89 meets Route 40 in this town.

23 Your last stop in the U.S. on the way to Mexico on Route 19 is at _____.

Down

2 Interstate highways are usually _____ than state highways.

3 On the border of California along Route 8 is which town?

5 If you go north from Phoenix on Route 17, you will meet Route 40 in _____.

7 Route 19 will take you south to which country?

8 If you drove west on Route 10 from Phoenix you would cross into which state?

9 This map would be useful if you travel by _____.

10 A highway that goes from state to state is called an _____.

11 Route 69 meets Route 89 in _____.

13 If you drove southwest from Wilcox on Route 10, this is the first town you would hit.

14 If you travel from Tucson to Nogales, in which direction will you be traveling?

16 Route 15 crosses into Arizona from the west from which state?

17 Interstate highways with even numbers go from east to _____.

19 Route 17 runs from south to _____.

21 Take Route 93 from Kingman to go for a swim in Lake _____.

DID YOU KNOW?

Today there are more than 42,000 miles of interstate highways in the United States. The interstate highway system was started by the federal government in 1944.

Temperature

Florida

One of the most important parts of climate is temperature. Temperature is usually measured in degrees Fahrenheit, but it can also be measured in degrees Celsius. In areas where there are changing seasons it is often useful to have two different temperature maps: one for summer and one for winter. The maps on this page show the average daily temperatures throughout Florida during January and July.

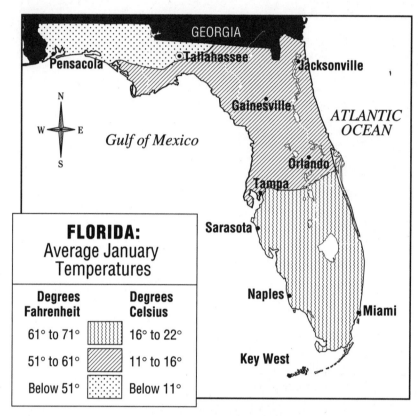

FLORIDA:
Average January
Temperatures

Degrees Fahrenheit		Degrees Celsius
61° to 71°		16° to 22°
51° to 61°		11° to 16°
Below 51°		Below 11°

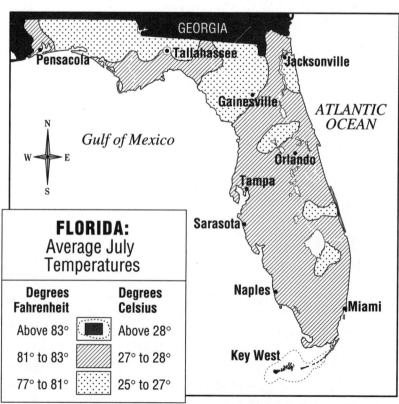

FLORIDA:
Average July
Temperatures

Degrees Fahrenheit		Degrees Celsius
Above 83°		Above 28°
81° to 83°		27° to 28°
77° to 81°		25° to 27°

DID YOU KNOW?

Every year three times as many people visit Florida as tourists than live there year round. Florida produces 8 out of every 10 oranges grown in the United States.

Temperature

NOTE:
Clues use degrees
fahrenheit

Across

1 These maps show temperatures of what place?

4 The most western city in Florida below 51° in January.

8 July is in which season?

11 In July, the temperature in Key West is _____ 83°.

12 Just north of Florida is which state?

15 Temperature can be measured in degrees Fahrenheit or _____.

16 Florida's capital city, _____, is in the coolest part of the state.

18 The temperature of Tallahassee is _____ 51° in January.

20 Winds from the _____ Ocean cool eastern Florida in summer.

22 In the United States, we usually measure temperature in degrees _____.

23 In summer, Key West is _____ than Gainesville.

Down

2 This city is between 51° and 61° in winter, warm enough for Mickey Mouse to go out without a coat.

3 The top map shows temperatures in which month?

5 In the _____ part of Florida, winter temperatures are cooler.

6 The bottom map shows temperatures in which month?

7 If you want to visit the hottest place in Florida, go to _____.

9 These are the units for measuring temperature.

10 The temperature of this southern Florida city is between 81° and 83° in summer and 61° to 71° in winter.

13 As you move north in winter, the temperature is _____.

14 Florida's warm temperatures make it a good place to go on _____.

16 This city is right on the edge of two different January temperature areas.

17 As you move in which direction does the temperature become hotter?

18 The temperature in Tampa in July is _____ 81° and 83°.

19 January is in which season?

21 The temperature in Florida is just one part of its _____.

Vegetation

World

A vegetation map shows which kinds of plants grow in an area. A vegetation map for a garden, for example, might show where roses and tulips grow. The map on this page shows the vegetation of the entire world. Since there are more than 400,000 types of plants in the world, they can not all be shown on this map. For that reason, this map is divided into major vegetation areas, providing a general idea of which kinds of plants grow in a place.

Name _____

North Pacific Ocean

AUSTRALIA

ASIA

Arctic Ocean

Indian Ocean

N
W   E
S

EUROPE

AFRICA

South Atlantic Ocean

ANTARCTICA

North Atlantic Ocean

Arctic Ocean

NORTH AMERICA

SOUTH AMERICA

North Pacific Ocean

South Pacific Ocean

VEGETATION: World

■ Forest	Tundra	
▨ Grassland	Ice-covered land	
⬚ Desert	Oceans, lakes	

Vegetation

Across

2 Most of the earth is covered by _____, where the vegetation is under water.

6 The central area of the United States, the Great Plains, is which vegetation area?

9 There is _____ forest in South America than any other vegetation.

11 Most of Canada is covered by which vegetation?

14 The central part of this continent has much grassland.

17 The _____ part of the United States is forest land.

18 In the desert, the climate is _____.

21 Forest areas are filled with _____.

23 This small continent is almost all forest land.

24 Much of Greenland is covered by this cold stuff.

26 A desert fills the center of this southern continent.

Down

1 _____ the North Pole, there is lots of tundra and ice.

3 This continent has almost no vegetation; it is mostly ice.

4 In the center of this continent is a large area of tundra.

5 A large desert area is found in the _____ U.S.

7 The _____ part of Africa is covered by desert.

8 This continent has a long skinny area of tundra along its western coast.

10 Across the _____ of Africa is a large patch of grassland.

12 The _____ regions are found in very cold or high areas of the earth.

13 These are some of the driest and hottest regions of the earth.

15 You might find these animals with antlers in tundra areas.

16 Along the _____ of many oceans, there are many forest areas.

19 There is _____ desert area in North America than in Africa.

20 Grassland is good land for growing _____.

22 If you traveled _____ from the grassland of North America, you would reach desert.

25 If you walk _____ from the desert area in Africa, you will reach forest land.

DID YOU KNOW?

The word *tundra* comes from a Finnish word that means "barren land." Actually the tundra is home to many different types of vegetation: mosses, grasses, and lichen. Tundra animals include lemmings, reindeer, and polar bears.

Growth of Railroads

Europe

New ways of transportation cause a ripple-effect of changes in other parts of society. This map is a combination of a transportation map and a historical map: it shows how railroads grew in Europe in the 1800s. As the railroads spread, the movement of goods and people changed Europe in many ways.

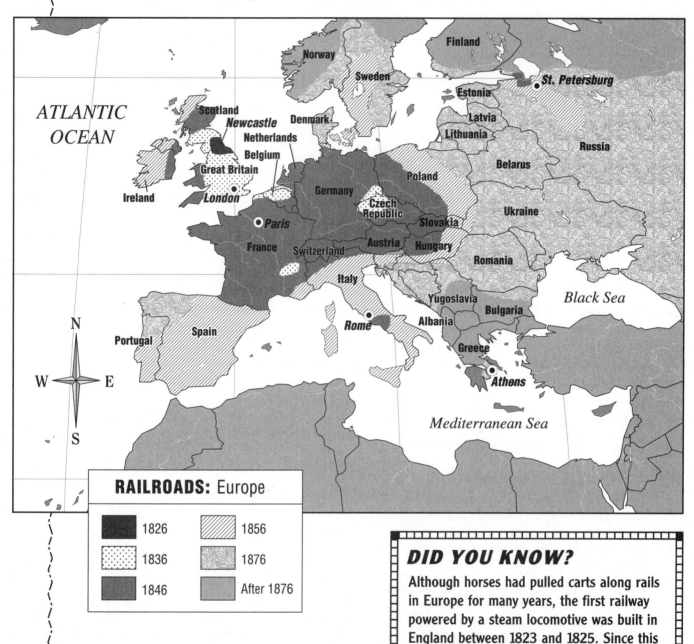

RAILROADS: Europe

■ 1826	▨ 1856		
⦂ 1836	≈ 1876		
▦ 1846	▧ After 1876		

DID YOU KNOW?

Although horses had pulled carts along rails in Europe for many years, the first railway powered by a steam locomotive was built in England between 1823 and 1825. Since this engine was built from iron, people began to call the locomotive the "iron horse."

Growth of Railroads

Across

3 Railroads were used to transport things to buildings where goods were made, called _____.

5 The _____ part of Great Britain was the last area to get railroads.

7 This country, Spain's neighbor, did not get railroads in the north until 1876.

9 First country in Scandinavia (Sweden, Norway, Denmark) to have railroads.

10 The first railroads in Britain were built around this city.

12 _____ 1826 there were no railroads in Europe.

13 The first railroads were built in England which is part of _____ _____.

18 Railroads provided a faster way to move goods and _____.

19 This map shows the growth of railroads in which continent?

21 Italy's first railroads were built close to the city of _____.

22 This map shows changes over how many years?

24 The last railroads on this map were built _____ 1876.

25 This map shows the growth of _____ in Europe.

Down

1 Railroads in the _____ part of Ireland were built in 1856.

2 In 1836 the first railroads were built in the northern tip of this country.

3 This part of the "boot" of Italy was the last to get railroads.

6 The _____ part was one of the last areas of Europe to get railroads.

8 Railroads did not provide a way to travel across _____.

11 This city in Russia had a railroad by 1846.

14 In 1846 there were no railroads south of the _____ between France and Spain.

15 The eastern part of this island got rails before the western part did.

16 Most of this country's railroads were made by 1856.

17 _____ was one of the countries in mainland Europe to build railroads by 1826.

20 This big country to the east was one of the last to build railroads.

23 This Mediterranean country was one of the last in Europe to get railroads.

Land Use

Colorado

One of the most common kind of maps is a land use map. These maps show how the land in a particular area is used for economic purposes. For example, land use maps show whether an area is used for farming or for manufacturing. This map shows the different ways land is used in the state of Colorado.

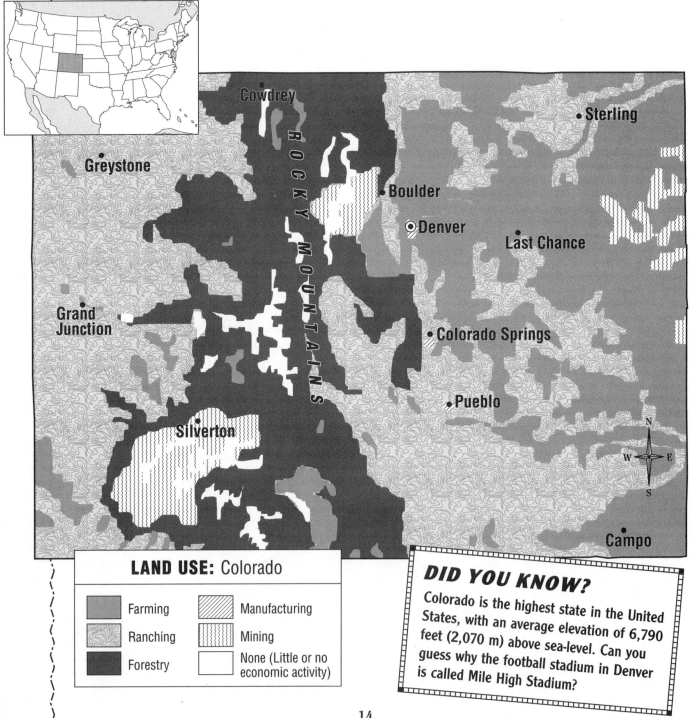

LAND USE: Colorado

Farming	Manufacturing
Ranching	Mining
Forestry	None (Little or no economic activity)

DID YOU KNOW?

Colorado is the highest state in the United States, with an average elevation of 6,790 feet (2,070 m) above sea-level. Can you guess why the football stadium in Denver is called Mile High Stadium?

Land Use

Across

3 Much of the land in the middle of Colorado is used for _____.

6 In manufacturing areas, many people work in what kind of buildings?

7 You are likely to see many of these animals in ranching areas.

8 Much of the land in western Colorado is used for _____.

11 Land where people dig for minerals is used for _____.

17 There is a lot of ranching around this west Colorado town.

21 Northeast town located in a ranching area.

22 _____ are the important resource for the forest industry.

23 This is the most southern manufacturing area in Colorado.

24 This city is the biggest center for manufacturing.

Down

1 Land use of an area helps determine what kind of _____ people have there.

2 Important resources in farming areas include good soil and plenty of _____.

4 Ranching is the largest land use area. Manufacturing is the _____.

5 The area around the _____ Mountains is used for forestry.

9 Areas where there is little economic activity are listed on this map as _____.

10 This north-central Colorado town has forests nearby.

11 Colorado Springs is one of three cities in the state where land is used for _____.

12 Land in Last Chance is used for what?

13 This town is located in a mining area. It's name sounds like a precious metal.

14 In mining areas, workers take minerals from _____ the ground.

15 There are more cattle than people in some areas near this northwest Colorado town.

16 Manufacturing areas are not in the country, but in _____.

18 Land is used for farming in this town in the southeast.

19 The land used for farming is not hilly, but rather _____.

20 Most of the _____ part of Colorado is used for farming.

Products

Montana

A product map shows the products, or goods, that are made in a place. This map shows some of the important products in the state of Montana. It is a useful way to learn about the relationship between the geography and economy of a place.

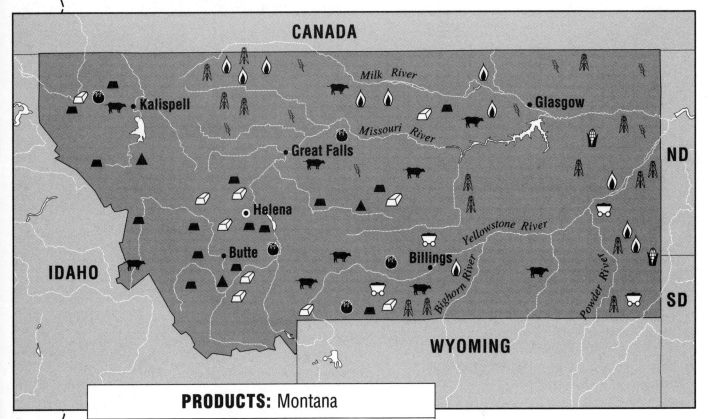

PRODUCTS: Montana

🐂 Cattle	🌽 Corn	🔥 Natural gas
🛒 Coal	◇ Gold	⚒ Petroleum (oil)
▲ Poultry	🍅 Vegetables	◉ State capital
■ Silver	🌾 Wheat	• City

DID YOU KNOW?

The name *Montana* comes from a Spanish word meaning "mountainous region." The coldest temperature ever recorded in the lower 48 states was in Rogers Pass, Montana: -70° F (-57°C) in 1954.

Name _____

Products

Across

4 Western town with cattle and gold nearby.

6 This town in northeast Montana has wheat fields nearby.

7 City by a river with cattle ranches east of it.

8 Crop that can be eaten right off the cob.

14 Rivers can be used for _____ or for moving products from place to place.

16 This product is sometimes known as "black gold."

18 This city in southern Montana has vegetables nearby.

20 The cow symbol stands for which product?

21 The _____ River runs by the city of Billings.

23 Even a little bit of this product is worth a lot of money.

24 Gold and silver make Montana's capital city _____, a rich town.

25 Most corn is grown in the _____ part of the state.

Down

1 The _____ River runs across the state into North Dakota.

2 Most silver and gold are found in the _____ part of Montana.

3 Natural gas and _____ are often found near each other.

5 Another word for farming.

9 This Montana product is used to make bread and cookies.

10 This black rock is burned to make electricity.

11 The products of a place often determine what kinds of _____ people do there.

12 People who dig gold and silver work in _____.

13 A triangle shows where _____ is an important product.

15 The flame symbol stands for which product?

17 A black block is the symbol for _____.

18 If you are a golddigger, you might like to live in _____.

19 Oil and natural gas are often found _____ one another.

22 Where there is poultry there will always be _____.

Precipitation

Africa

A precipitation map shows the amount of snow, rain, sleet, and hail that falls to the earth in a place in an average. The greater the precipitation in a place, the wetter it is. Precipitation is one of the most important parts of climate, and it can have a great effect on the way people in a place live. For example, the crops people grow depend a great deal on the precipitation where they live.

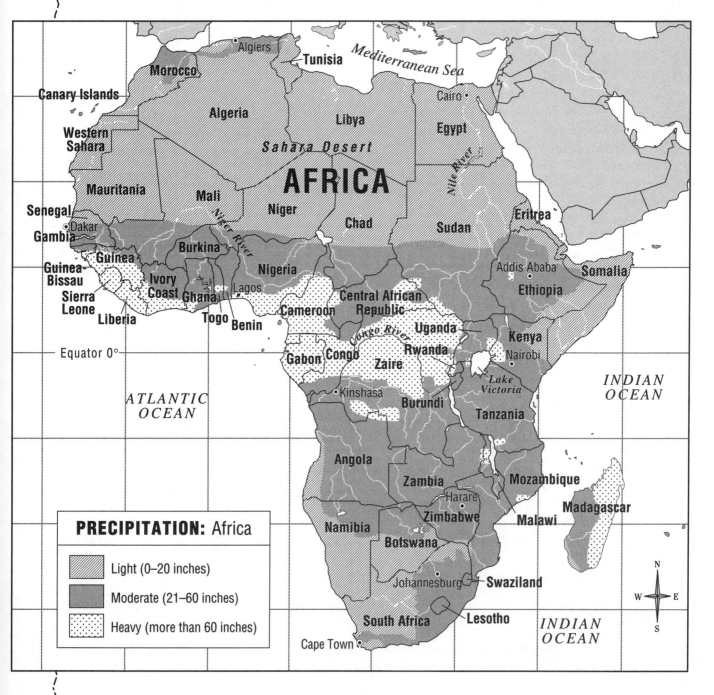

PRECIPITATION: Africa

Light (0–20 inches)

Moderate (21–60 inches)

Heavy (more than 60 inches)

Precipitation

Across

3 The large lake near the center of Africa is Lake _____.

4 Along this line of 0° latitude, called the _____, are some of Africa's wettest areas.

7 Another word for rain and snow is _____.

8 This very southern city is in an area of moderate rainfall.

11 Gabon receives _____ rain than Egypt.

14 Most of the coast along the _____ Sea is very dry.

19 Areas that receive 0-20 inches of precipitation are called _____ in the key.

20 Annual precipitation means the amount of rain that falls in one _____.

21 The Nile River flows right by this Egyptian city.

22 Areas with heavy precipitation are _____.

23 This island off Africa has all three precipitation areas.

24 This river carries water from Central Africa to the Atlantic.

Down

1 This capital city of Kenya is in a moderate precipitation area.

2 Landform often found in very dry areas.

5 North African country completely in a light precipitation area.

6 This Central African country is one of the wettest in Africa.

9 This city is in one of the few areas with moderate rainfall in North Africa.

10 Most of _____ Africa is very dry.

11 Areas that receive between 21 and 60 inches of precipitation are called _____ in the key.

12 Farming, also called _____, is difficult in areas with light precipitation.

13 Areas that receive more than 60 inches of precipitation are considered _____ in the key.

15 Along the coast of this ocean are some wet areas.

16 This mighty river flows north from Central Africa to the Mediterranean Sea.

17 The amount of rain that falls can affect the type of plants that grow, called _____.

18 This country in East Africa has all three types of precipitation areas.

21 The northern part of the country of _____ is dry; the southern part has moderate rainfall.

DID YOU KNOW?

The Sahara Desert is the largest desert in the world. It covers more than 3.5 million square miles, more than ten times the size of Texas. Some parts of this dry land receive no precipitation for years at a time.

City Map
London

Imagine that you have taken a vacation to London, England. London today is a big, bustling city of 6 million people. To find your way around London, a city map will certainly come in handy. The map below shows a part of central London and highlights important streets and bridges, as well as subway stations, information booths, and tourist attractions.

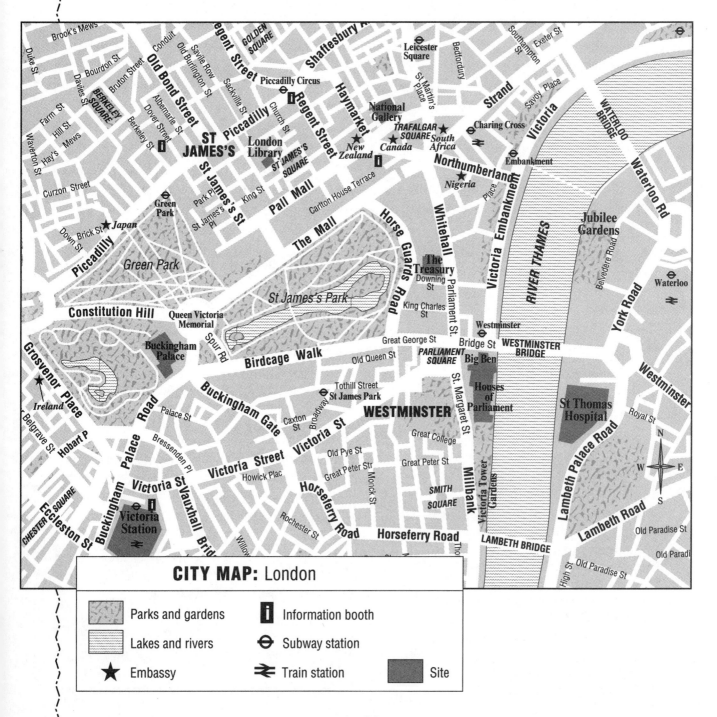

CITY MAP: London

- Parks and gardens
- Lakes and rivers
- ★ Embassy
- **i** Information booth
- ⊖ Subway station
- ⇌ Train station
- ◼ Site

City Map

Across

4 Along the _____ Walk you might see birds in St. James's Park.

9 Off St. James's Square you can check out a book at London _____.

10 After visiting the Jubilee Gardens, catch the subway at _____.

12 To cross the Thames River, you could swim or take the Westminster _____.

13 Victoria _____ is located near Buckingham Palace Road.

18 The "i" symbol stands for what?

20 You can go for a boat ride in the pond in St. James's _____.

21 The embassy of _____ is north of St. James's Park, near Trafalgar Square.

22 On a rainy day, you might want to travel underground on the _____.

23 This famous big clock is found near the Houses of Parliament.

24 British laws are made in the Houses of _____.

Down

1 If you lived in _____, your embassy would be on Northumberland Avenue.

2 This river cuts through the heart of London.

3 At the end of the Mall is a memorial to Queen _____.

5 A big museum on Trafalgar Square is the National _____.

6 If you like traveling underground, you can pick up the subway at Charing _____.

7 Drive straight up Great George Street to cross the Thames at _____ Bridge.

8 If you worked in the Houses of Parliament, you could look south to see the Victoria Tower _____.

11 This park's name is also its color.

12 The Queen's house is called _____ Palace.

14 The embassy of _____ is on Grosvenor Place.

15 If you're feeling sick along Lambeth Palace Road, stop in at St. Thomas' _____.

16 North of Green Park is a funny sounding street.

17 The British Government keeps money in the _____ along Whitehall.

19 The most southern bridge on this map is the _____ Bridge.

DID YOU KNOW?

London was founded way back in AD 43 by the Romans. They called it *Londoninium*.

Indian Culture Areas

North America

Before the first Europeans arrived in North America, millions of Native Americans, or Indians, lived across the continent. They made up more than 1,000 different cultures, with widely different customs, languages, and ways of life. This map shows some of the major culture groups using shaded areas. Specific groups are labeled directly on the map.

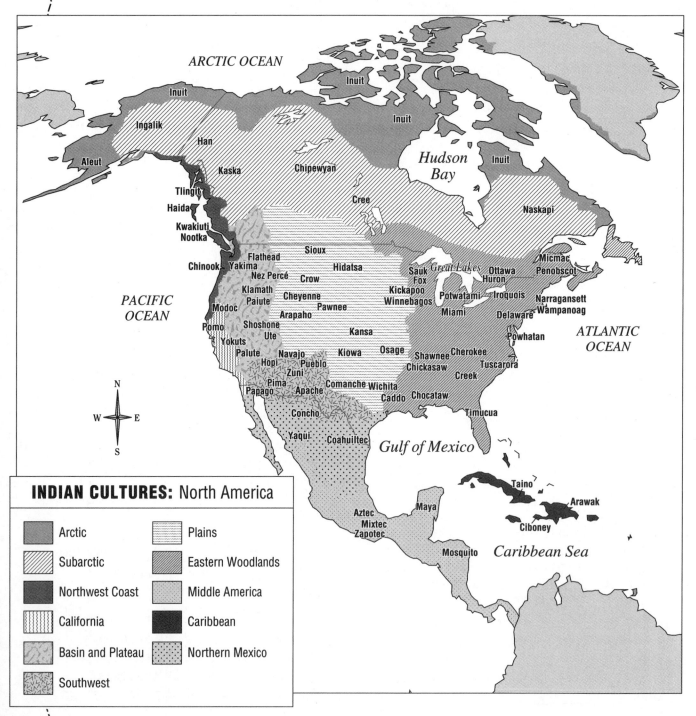

ARCTIC OCEAN

Inuit
Inuit
Inuit
Inuit
Ingalik
Han
Aleut
Kaska
Chipewyan
Hudson Bay
Inuit
Tlingit
Haida
Cree
Naskapi
Kwakiutl
Nootka
Chinook
Flathead
Yakima
Sioux
Hidatsa
Great Lakes
Sauk
Fox
Ottawa
Huron
Micmac
Penobscot
Nez Percé
Crow
Kickapoo
Potwatami
Iroquois
Narragansett
Klamath
Paiute
Cheyenne
Winnebagos
Miami
Delaware
Wampanoag
Modoc
Pawnee
PACIFIC OCEAN
Arapaho
Pomo
Shoshone
Kansa
Powhatan
ATLANTIC OCEAN
Yokuts
Ute
Palute
Navajo
Kiowa
Osage
Shawnee
Cherokee
Hopi
Pueblo
Chickasaw
Tuscarora
Zuni
Creek
Pima
Comanche
Wichita
Papago
Apache
Caddo
Chocataw
Concho
Timucua
Yaqui
Coahuiltec
Gulf of Mexico
Taino
Arawak
Aztec
Maya
Mixtec
Zapotec
Ciboney
Mosquito
Caribbean Sea

N W E S

INDIAN CULTURES: North America

- Arctic
- Subarctic
- Northwest Coast
- California
- Basin and Plateau
- Southwest
- Plains
- Eastern Woodlands
- Middle America
- Caribbean
- Northern Mexico

Indian Culture Areas

Across

1 Living near the Shawnee and Tuscarora in the Southeast were the _____.

5 This group lived in present-day California.

7 The name of this group of Southwest Indians comes from the Spanish word for "village."

10 Along the coast north of California were the _____ Coast cultures.

11 The Pomo were part of which Indian culture?

12 The Paiute, Klamath, and Shoshone were all part of this culture.

16 In the flat area at the center of the United States lived the _____ cultures.

17 These people lived in the very southeastern tip of the United States.

19 The eastern part of the United States was home to the Eastern _____ cultures.

21 The Ottawa, Huron, and Sauk lived near which huge bodies of water?

22 The Indian group which lived in the far north.

23 The Tlingit used the _____ Ocean as a source of food.

24 This group lived in the present-day state of Maine.

Down

2 One of the Great Lakes is named after this group.

3 The Timucua lived in the present-day state of _____.

4 The environment of the Eastern Woodlands was mostly _____.

6 The Pima and Hopi were part of which culture?

8 These people lived in western Alaska.

9 A state in the center of the United States takes its name from the people named _____.

11 This group that lived in the northern plains has the same name as a bird.

13 The Narragansett Indians fished in this ocean.

14 A state is named after this Eastern Woodland group.

15 This region of Indian cultures means "below arctic."

18 These Indians lived near the border of Mexico.

20 This group lived near the Great Lakes, but now there is a city in Florida with its name.

DID YOU KNOW?

Among the many crops first grown by Native Americans were tomatoes, potatoes, artichokes, and squashes.

Climate

Europe

Climate maps show what the weather of a place is like over a period of time. They show the patterns of weather, such as hot, dry summers or cold, wet winters. This map shows the many different climate zones of Europe, which has great variety in spite of the continent's small size.

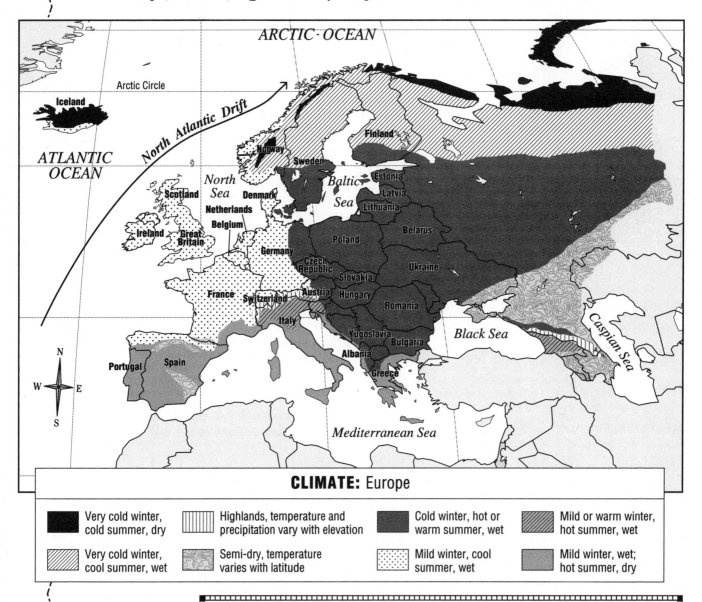

CLIMATE: Europe

■ Very cold winter, cold summer, dry	▥ Highlands, temperature and precipitation vary with elevation	▨ Cold winter, hot or warm summer, wet	▧ Mild or warm winter, hot summer, wet
▨ Very cold winter, cool summer, wet	▨ Semi-dry, temperature varies with latitude	⋮ Mild winter, cool summer, wet	▨ Mild winter, wet; hot summer, dry

DID YOU KNOW?

A current of warm water in the Atlantic Ocean called the North Atlantic Drift helps to moderate the climate of much of Europe. This warming current explains why the weather in London, England, is much more mild than that in Calgary, Canada, even though these two cities are at about the same latitude.

Climate

Across

1 As you head in this direction, the climate is usually warmer.

5 Along this sea, summers are hot and dry.

11 These bodies of water carry rain to the sea.

12 Above the line called the Arctic _____, it is cold all the time.

13 Sometimes this inland northern sea freezes so that you can skate on it!

14 This country, near the center of Europe, has mild winters.

16 A big word that means moisture that falls to earth.

18 "Climate" is the word we use to describe the _____ of a place over time.

Down

1 During this season, the weather in much of Finland is cool and wet.

2 Summer in the south of Spain is _____.

3 The North Atlantic _____ brings warm water toward Europe.

4 Along the _____ coast of Europe, the weather is wet and mild most of the year.

6 If you like hot summers, you might get a kick out of visiting this boot-shaped country.

7 These tall mountains are covered with snow year round.

8 Even in summer, it is cold in the extreme _____ of Europe.

9 The climate on this island is so cold, its name even sounds chilly.

10 In southern Sweden, the season of _____ is cold.

15 Winters in northern Spain are _____.

17 Air blown from this ocean warms the British Isles.

Name _____

Physical
Antarctica

The continent of Antarctica was the last continent to be accurately mapped. It was difficult because it lies under snow and ice that in some places is more than a mile thick. Still, this frozen land mass at the bottom of the earth has many interesting features, from ice shelves to glaciers. It also has interesting wildlife, such as penguins and seals.

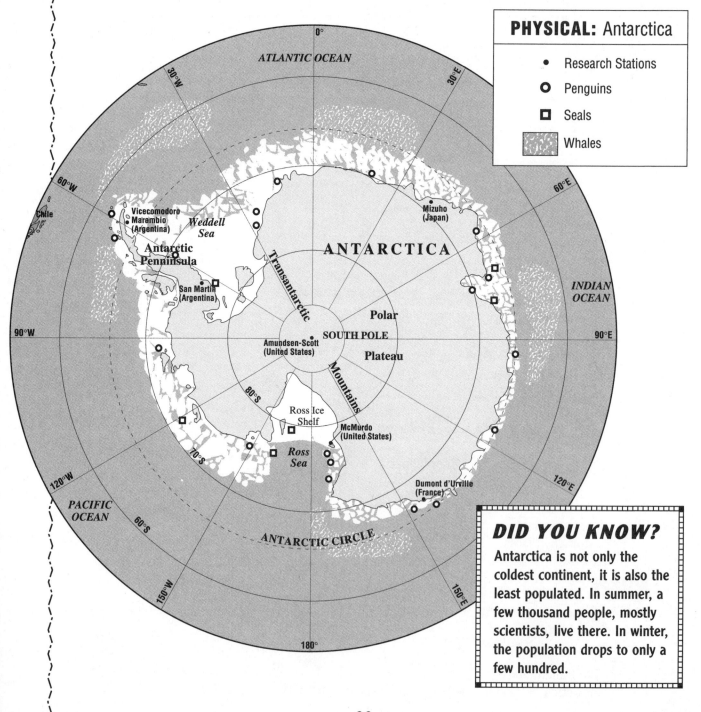

PHYSICAL: Antarctica
- • Research Stations
- ○ Penguins
- □ Seals
- Whales

DID YOU KNOW?

Antarctica is not only the coldest continent, it is also the least populated. In summer, a few thousand people, mostly scientists, live there. In winter, the population drops to only a few hundred.

Physical

Across

2 The San Martin Station is operated by this country.

4 The high flat area of land called the Polar_____ is near the middle of the continent.

6 Crossing Antarctica are the tall Transantarctic _____.

9 Lines of _____ all meet at the South Pole.

11 The line of latitude at about 66ºS which marks the beginning of a very cold area, is called the Antarctic _____.

13 This country has a station right at the South Pole.

17 It seems like the season of _____ year-round in Antarctica.

19 Even during the summer, the weather in Antarctica is _____.

21 These large sheets of ice cover large parts of Antarctica.

22 The Antarctic Peninsula borders the _____ Sea.

23 These huge swimming mammals are found off the coast in many places.

24 These tuxedo-wearing birds are found near the Ross Sea.

Down

1 This continent is located further south than any other.

2 The Pacific, Indian, and _____ Oceans border Antarctica.

3 At the opposite end of the earth from the South Pole is the _____.

5 This American station is near the Ross Sea.

7 There is plenty of this material, made of frozen water, in Antarctica.

8 This finger-shaped landform is surrounded by water on three sides.

10 The southernmost spot on earth is called the _____.

11 This is the closest country to Antarctica.

12 This island country has a station called "Mizuho."

14 The Ross Ice _____ is a flat area frozen year-round.

15 A common form of precipitation in Antarctica.

16 The Dumont D'Urville station was set up by which country?

18 This large floating chunk of ice can mean danger for ships sailing to Antarctica.

20 These big swimming creatures can be seen along the Weddell Sea.

Scale

Kansas

Scale is the relationship between distances shown on a map and the real distances on earth. Maps with larger scale, such as Map B, show more detail than maps with smaller scale, such as Map A. The scale of a map is shown by a straight line divided that tell how many miles or kilometers equals one inch. Using this scale, you can measure a distance on a map and then figure out the real distance in miles or kilometers on earth. You will need a ruler to answer some of the questions in this puzzle.

Map A

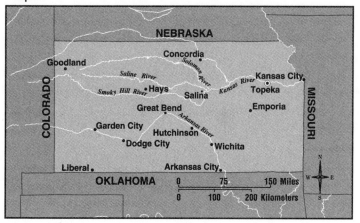

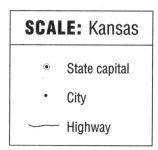

Map B

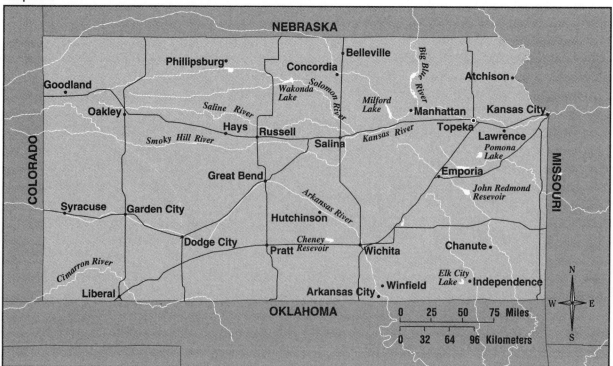

Scale

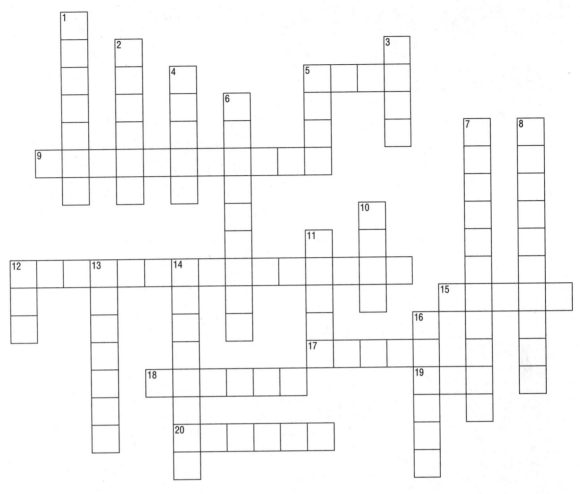

Across

5 If you need a quick picture of Kansas without much detail, which map would you use?

9 On Map B one inch equals _____ miles.

12 On Map A, one inch equals _____ miles.

15 A map is a picture of a real place on _____.

17 The _____ on a map is used to figure the real distance on earth.

18 Both maps show the state of _____.

19 The distance on Map B from Russell to Goodland is about _____ inches, which equals 150 miles.

20 The dots on both maps stand for _____.

Down

1 Map A is _____ than Map B.

2 Map B is _____ than Map A.

3 If you wanted the most information about Kansas highways, which map would you use?

4 The north pointer on Map A points in which direction?

5 A map with bigger scale is able to show _____ detail.

6 These two maps have _____ scales.

7 A large-scale map can give more _____ than a small-scale map.

8 The scales on the maps are shown in both miles and _____.

10 _____ of these maps show the state of Kansas.

11 The scales on these maps are listed in both kilometers and _____.

12 On Map B, how many inches equals 75 miles?

13 A black line on Map B stands for a _____.

14 A map scale is used to measure the _____ from one place to another.

16 Since Map B is bigger, it shows more _____.

DID YOU KNOW?

The oldest map in the world, a clay tablet from 3000 B.C. showing a farm in ancient Sumer, (present-day Iraq), includes a scale.

Name _____

Endangered Species
Africa

Endangered species are animals and plants that are in danger of disappearing
from earth. This map shows where four of the endangered species in Africa live.
Altogether there are more than 900 animals and 400 plants that are listed as
endangered or threatened in the world. By studying these animals and plants and
their environments, scientists can better work to protect them from extinction.

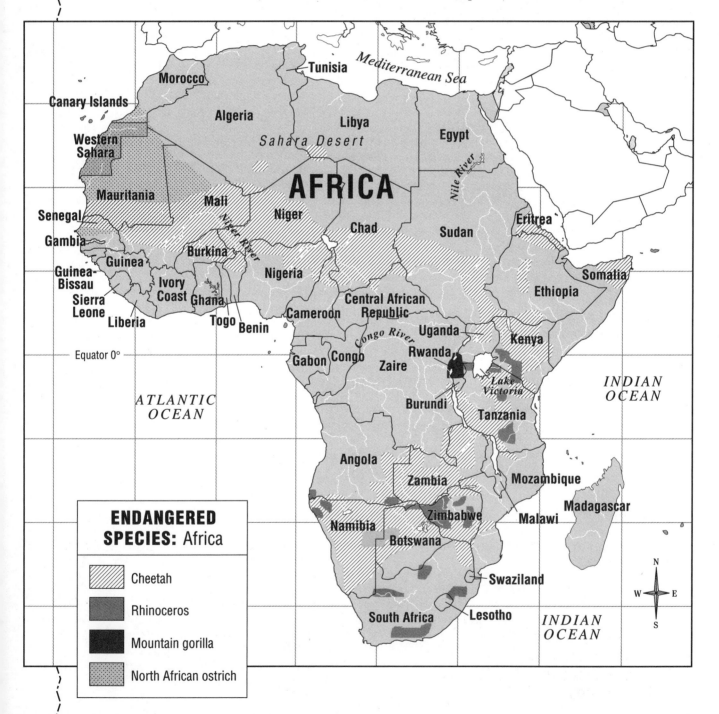

Endangered Species

Across

1 None of the four endangered animals live on this island off the coast of East Africa.

3 The cheetah ranges through most of this West African country.

5 This country is the most northern place where the cheetah is found.

9 The most southern country where the rhino roams.

11 The cheetah and the rhinoceros are _____ found in Tanzania.

14 The cheetah has the _____ range of these animals.

15 The most eastern country where the cheetah is found is _____.

16 This southwestern country has both cheetahs and rhinos.

18 The range of the cheetah runs along the border of which desert?

19 The gorilla has the _____ range of these animals.

20 Both rhinos and cheetahs are found along the shores of which lake?

21 The _____ is a kind of big cat.

Down

1 The North African ostrich goes no further east than this country.

2 This large animal is scattered through south and east Africa.

4 None of these four animals are found in this country of North Africa.

6 An ostrich is what kind of animal?

7 The ostrich is found throughout this entire country.

8 The mountain _____ has the smallest range of these four animals.

9 You can tell a cheetah by what pattern on its fur.

10 This map shows how many different endangered species?

12 The range of the cheetah is mostly _____ the equator.

13 Gorillas live in the southern part of this country.

17 This species is found only in northwestern Africa.

DID YOU KNOW?

The cheetah is the fastest animal on earth, capable of reaching speeds of 70 miles per hour, faster than the speed limit on most highways.

Religions
World

Some maps give information not just about a place but also about the people who live there. This map shows the major religions of the world. It gives a picture of where the people who follow these different religions live. A map like this is useful for learning about the culture of a place.

RELIGIONS: World

Christianity	Confucianism, Daoism, and Buddhism
Islam	Shinto and Buddhism
Hinduism	Other
Buddhism	✡ Judaism

North Pacific Ocean

AUSTRALIA

Japan

China

ASIA

Arctic Ocean

Russia

Indian Ocean

N
E
W
S

Saudi Arabia

Somalia

Sudan

EUROPE

AFRICA

Zaire

South Africa

Libya

Algeria

ANTARCTICA

North Atlantic Ocean

South Atlantic Ocean

Brazil

SOUTH AMERICA

Argentina

Chile

Canada

NORTH AMERICA

U.S.A.

Mexico

North Pacific Ocean

South Pacific Ocean

Arctic Ocean

DID YOU KNOW?

Christianity is the most popular religion in the world today, with nearly 2 billion believers. Islam is the second most popular, with about 1 billion believers.

Religions

Across

1 In this part of Asia, Confucianism is popular.

4 As you move further _____ in Asia, there are more people who follow Christianity.

5 This small continent has many Christians, but also followers of Islam and Judaism.

8 Japan is the only country where the _____ religion is practiced.

10 Shinto and Buddhism are the main religions on this island nation.

12 This is the world's most popular religion, found on every continent.

14 This continent has more different religions than any other.

15 In Asia there are many followers of _____ north of a large Hindu area.

16 Along this northern ocean, many people believe in their own native religions, marked "other."

17 Many Jews and Christians sailed across the _____ Ocean from Europe to settle in America.

19 This religion is popular in east Asia, especially China.

22 Many followers of Judaism live near _____, rather than in the countryside.

23 This is one country that has many people that follow the same religion.

24 This line of latitude runs across Christian areas of South America and Africa.

Down

2 Like its neighbor to the south, this continent has followers of Christianity, Judaism, and "other."

3 The country of India is made up mostly of people who follow _____.

6 In the _____ part of Asia, there are many followers of Buddhism and Islam.

7 The followers of _____ are scattered on many continents of the world.

9 The _____ part of Africa has many followers of Islam.

11 There are so few people here that there is no major religion.

13 This island continent has many Christians and "others."

18 A large area of this continent has followers of Islam.

20 Smaller religions that are different in different places are marked _____ on this map.

21 This religion is popular in northern Africa and southern Asia.

Comparing Maps
Baseball Teams, 1952 to 1995

Maps can even give interesting information about our national pastime, baseball. The maps on this page show the changes of the teams in the major leagues from 1952 to 1995. The changes detailed on these maps reflect many other changes in America, such as the movement of people from the eastern United States to the western part of the country.

COMPARING MAPS:
Baseball Teams

☆ Baseball team

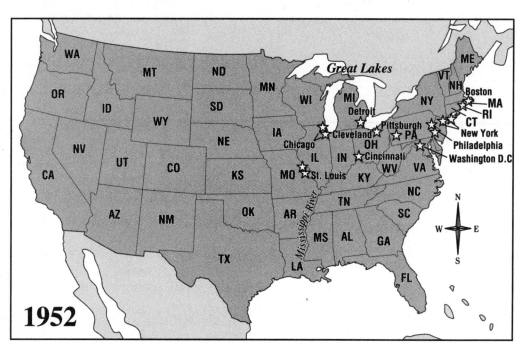

1952

DID YOU KNOW?

Many people think that baseball was invented by Abner Doubleday in 1839, but it's not true. In fact, baseball developed slowly from other ball games, such as cricket and rounders. The first official baseball game was played in Hoboken, New Jersey, in 1846.

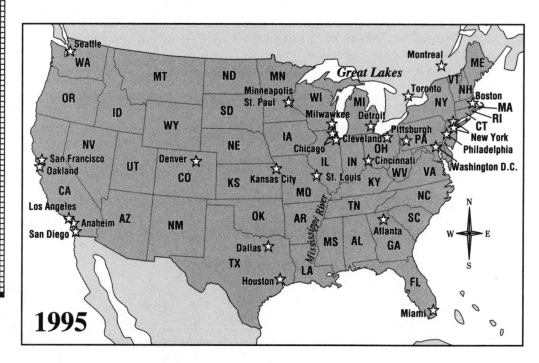

1995

Comparing Maps

Across

2 This western state has a team named after the nearby Rocky Mountains.

3 The team in this city is the closest to Mexico.

4 This state had no teams in 1952, but five in 1995.

5 This city in Michigan had a team in 1995 and 1952.

7 One team in Canada is in Montreal, the other is in _____.

9 How many teams were in California in 1995?

11 There were _____ teams in 1995 than in 1952.

13 This eastern state had three teams in 1952 and two teams in 1995.

14 This city in the Middle West is home to two teams.

16 The one team in Florida is in which city?

18 Most of the teams new since 1952 were not in the east, but in the _____.

19 The team in this Missouri city is only a toss away from the Mississippi River.

20 This big state had two teams in 1995.

21 Most baseball teams are not located in small towns, but in big _____.

Down

1 This northeast city had two teams in 1952 but only one in 1995.

2 Not all the teams are in the United States. There are two teams in which other country?

3 The team in the northwestern United States is in which city?

6 In 1995 there were how many teams west of the Mississippi River?

8 How many teams were in northern California in 1995?

10 In 1952 most baseball teams were in which region of the United States?

11 In 1952 there were only two teams west of this big river.

12 This state has a team named after the twin cities, Minneapolis and St. Paul.

13 In 1952 there were no teams along the coast of which ocean?

15 Many teams are located around the _____ Lakes.

17 On the 1995 map there is a team in this Georgia city.

Subway
Washington, D.C., Metro

In many cities, subways are the fastest way to get around. Since they travel underground, subways don't get caught in traffic. This map shows the four routes of the Washington, D.C., subway, which is called the "Metro."

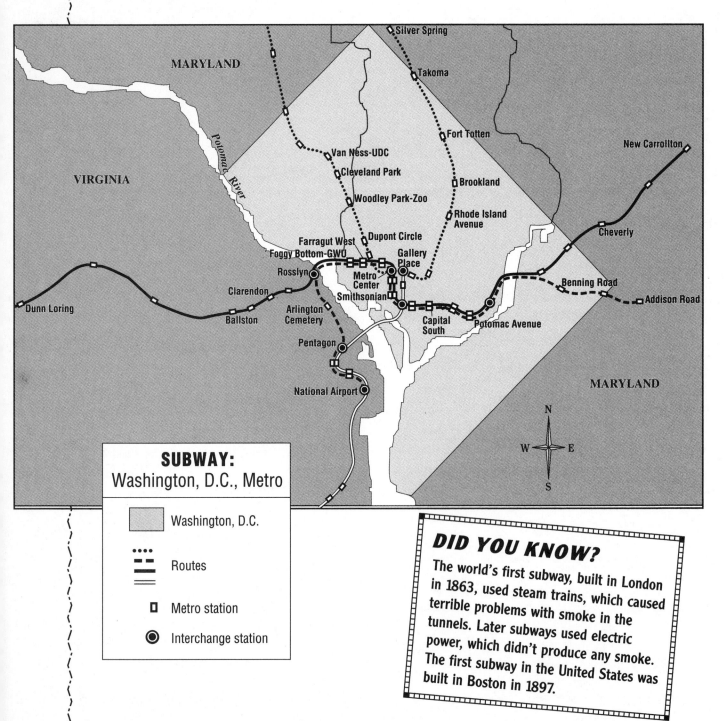

SUBWAY:
Washington, D.C., Metro

- Washington, D.C.
- ••• Routes
- ▫ Metro station
- ◉ Interchange station

DID YOU KNOW?

The world's first subway, built in London in 1863, used steam trains, which caused terrible problems with smoke in the tunnels. Later subways used electric power, which didn't produce any smoke. The first subway in the United States was built in Boston in 1897.

Subway

Across

2 The line that runs roughly east to west.

3 This map shows the subway system in which city?

7 The white line has a stop at _____.

8 The line that is shown by _____ begins at National Airport.

13 Both the white and dash line can take you to your airplane at _____.

14 At this station, you can change to the dot, dash, or the black line.

17 The line shown by _____ comes from the north and loops up again.

18 How many subway lines are there in Washington?

19 Three of the subway lines cross the _____ River.

20 People who take the subway west and south of the city go to the state of _____.

21 The last stop on the east end of the dash line is _____.

Down

1 New Carrollton station is the furthest in which direction?

4 The white line heads in which direction from the city?

5 A _____ stands for a station where you can change subway lines.

6 Dunn Loring is the station that is furthest _____ on the map.

9 A _____ is the symbol for an ordinary subway station.

10 Hop off at this station to visit the famous museum.

11 The end of the dot line is at _____.

12 You would get off at Woodley Park if you want to visit the animals at the _____.

14 This state is north and east of Washington, D.C.

15 All the subway lines come together at the _____ of Washington, D.C.

16 The dot line heads in which direction from the city?

Population

Europe

One kind of map that shows interesting information about people is a population map. Population maps show the number of people who live in a given area, usually a square mile or square kilometer. A city, for example, has greater population than a rural area. One glance at a population map will show you that cities are much more crowded than the countryside. The map below shows where the 500 million people of Europe call home.

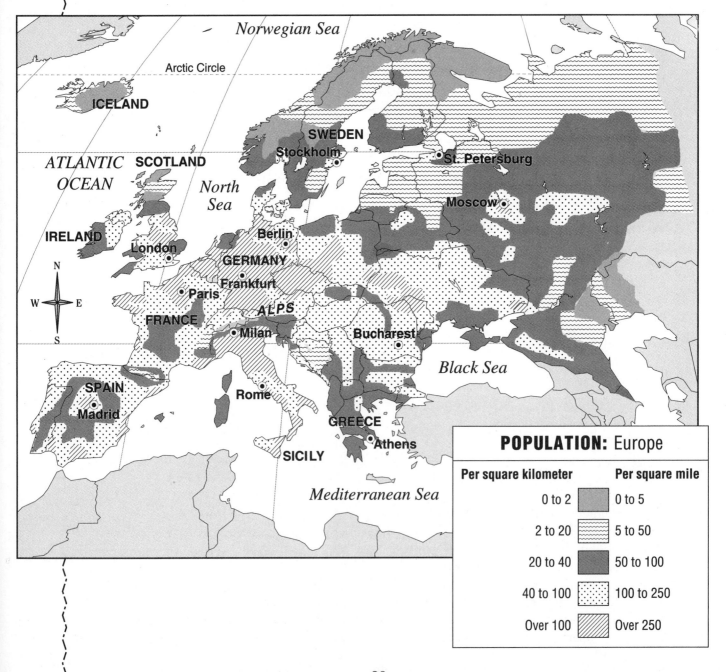

POPULATION: Europe

Per square kilometer		Per square mile
0 to 2		0 to 5
2 to 20		5 to 50
20 to 40		50 to 100
40 to 100		100 to 250
Over 100		Over 250

Population

Across

3 Very few people live above the _____ circle.

4 This is the most eastern city with population over 250 people per square mile.

6 As you move from east to _____ in Europe the population goes up.

7 A large area of high population runs across the _____ part of Europe.

10 The population around St. Petersburg is _____ than that around Berlin.

13 Population is the number of _____ that live in a place.

15 This German city is in the center of the high population area.

18 The northen part of this island has more people than the southern part.

19 This map shows which continent?

20 This island off Italy has more than 100 people per square mile.

22 In the center of Spain is this heavily populated city.

23 This country has the densest population in Europe.

24 The population of western Ireland is _____ 50 and 100 people per square mile.

25 The northern part of this part of Britain has 0 to 2 people per square kilometer.

Down

1 This map shows the number of people per square kilometer or per square _____.

2 Fewer people live in the _____ of Europe than in the south.

5 This boot-shaped country has more than 100 people per square mile.

8 Around this city in Greece the population is 50 to 100 people per square mile.

9 The _____ part of Sweden has more people than the northern part.

11 This Swedish city has between 100 and 250 people per square mile.

12 A thin band of low population north of Italy marks the location of what landforms?

14 The population of Rome is over one _____ people per square kilometer.

15 Much of Iceland has a population between zero and _____ people per square mile.

16 Along the coast of France by the _____ Ocean the population is high.

17 This island in the northern Atlantic has a small population.

21 This English city has many people living in it, more than 250 per square mile.

22 Is the area around Bucharest more or less crowded than the area around Athens?

DID YOU KNOW?

Most Europeans live in cities. In fact, in some countries, such as Belgium, more than nine out of ten people live in urban areas.

Historical Maps

North America

Historical maps show how a place has changed over time. You can use these maps to compare the way a place is now with the way it was years ago. The maps on this page show that the countries that controlled North America changed from 1713 to 1783. That was a long time ago, but these events still affect North America today. For example, people in Mexico speak Spanish, people in the United States speak English, and many people in Canada speak French. These languages came from the European settlers who claimed the land more than 300 years ago.

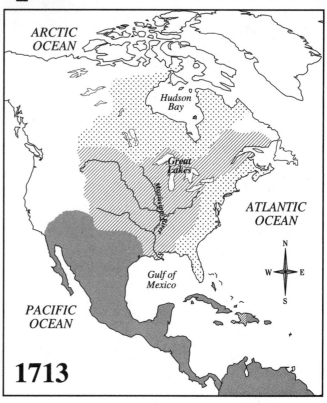

1713

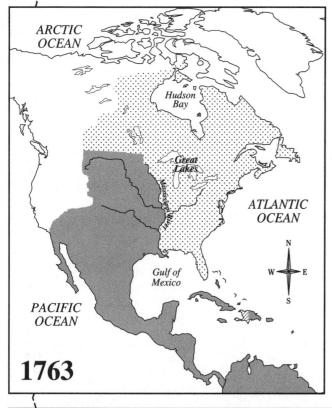

1763

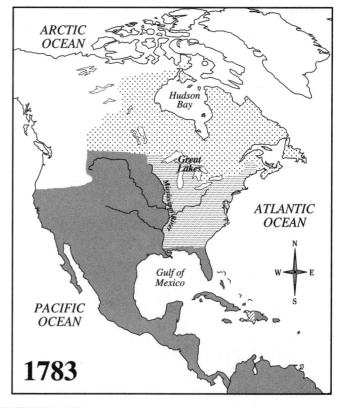

1783

CHANGING OWNERSHIP: North America

British   French   Spanish   Independent

Historical Maps

Across

3 In 1763 the British owned land mostly in the north and _____.

4 Between 1713 and 1763 which country lost most of its land?

8 The war that made an independent country in North America after 1783 was the American _____.

9 In 1783 did Spain control more or less of North America than in 1713?

12 Between 1763 and 1783 _____ lost much of its land in the east.

15 After 1783, Great Britain still controlled land in the _____.

16 In 1713 France owned most of the _____ part of North America.

19 These maps show the countries that controlled land in North _____.

20 These maps show changes of land ownership over _____.

21 In 1713 France owned land around the _____ Lakes.

23 In 1783 Spain controlled the land along the Pacific that is now the state of _____.

Down

1 In 1783 the eastern part of North America became _____.

2 In 1713 how much of North America was an independent country?

3 These countries that controlled land are on which continent?

4 Did France own more land in the first or last map?

5 The country listed as "independent" on the 1783 map is what country?

6 None of these countries claimed land in the far _____ part of the continent.

7 In 1783 Spain owned what is now the state of _____.

10 This country controlled the southern and western parts of North America in 1783.

11 In 1763 the border between Spanish and British land was the _____ River.

13 The British took land first along the coast of the _____ Ocean.

14 After 1763 how much land did France control in mainland North America?

17 Land along the _____ Ocean was claimed after that along the Atlantic.

18 In 1763 Spain owned land _____ of the Mississippi River.

22 Spain controlled the land of Mexico in _____ of these maps.

DID YOU KNOW?

Other countries also claimed land in North America, including Sweden, the Netherlands, and Russia.

Name _____

Natural Hazards

Australia and Oceania

One of the most exciting and frightening parts of geography is the natural hazard that appears suddenly, often causing tremendous damage. Volcanoes, earthquakes, tsunamis (tidal waves), and icebergs are examples, but even deserts can greatly change the landscape and the lives of people who live in a place. This map shows some of the natural hazards found in Australia and the islands that make up Oceania.

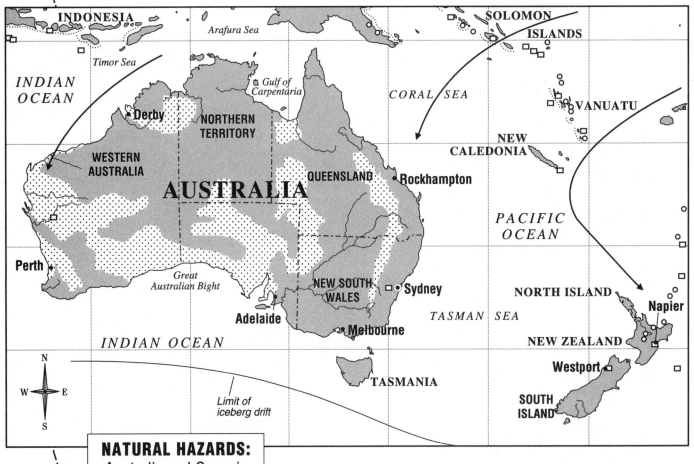

NATURAL HAZARDS:
Australia and Oceania

→ Tropical storm tracks

○ Volcanoes

□ Earthquakes

⁓ Tsunamis (tidal waves)

▦ Areas subject to desertification

DID YOU KNOW?

Australia is the world's smallest continent and also the driest. A greater part of Australia is desert than that of any other continent. In fact, only 6% of Australia's land can be used to grow crops.

Natural Hazards

Across

2 This is a kind of mountain that explodes.

4 An earthquake hit near this city on the North Island of New Zealand.

5 The city of Perth has this dry hazard nearby.

9 Northeast of Australia are the _____ Islands, which have earthquakes, volcanoes, and tsunamis.

12 This city in South Australia is near an area of desert.

13 There is much desert in this part of Australia.

14 An earthquake hit this city in South Island of New Zealand.

18 One tropical storm path heads right towards this Australia town.

22 In this northeastern region of Australia there have been no volcanoes or earthquakes.

23 The only country with desert hazards on this map.

24 This island south of Australia is quite close to the iceberg line.

Down

1 The most northern desert area is near which city in Northern Australia?

3 Which island of New Zealand has more volcanoes?

4 Most tropical storms come from which direction?

6 Australia's capital city, _____, had an earthquake nearby.

7 An earthquake occured off the southern tip of this island, New _____.

8 The _____ Island of New Zealand has had only one earthquake.

10 These islands near New Caledonia have had many volcanoes erupt nearby.

11 This shaky hazard has only happened in two places in Australia.

15 Powerful storms that come from the northeast are called _____ storms.

16 If you sailed south from Australia you might hit what floating hazard?

17 Western Australia borders which ocean?

19 This map shows natural _____.

20 Many tropical storms blow onto Australia from the _____ Sea.

21 This is another name for a tidal wave.

Transportation Routes

Colorado

Transportation maps show the routes that go from one place to another. These maps can show roads, railroads, steamship routes, airline routes, and even hiking trails. The transportation map on this page shows routes for three different forms of transportation in a section of the state of Colorado.

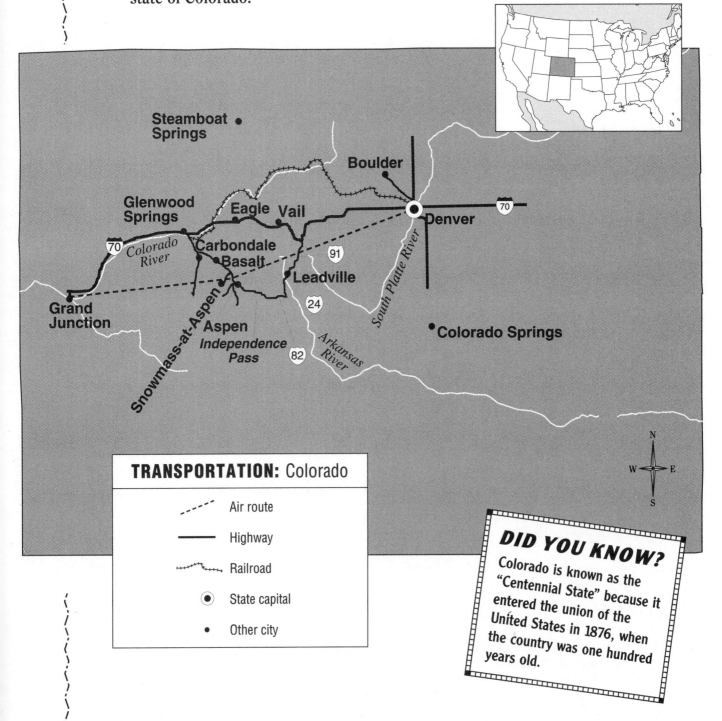

TRANSPORTATION: Colorado

- - - - - Air route

———— Highway

⌁⌁⌁⌁⌁ Railroad

◉ State capital

• Other city

DID YOU KNOW?

Colorado is known as the "Centennial State" because it entered the union of the United States in 1876, when the country was one hundred years old.

Transportation Routes

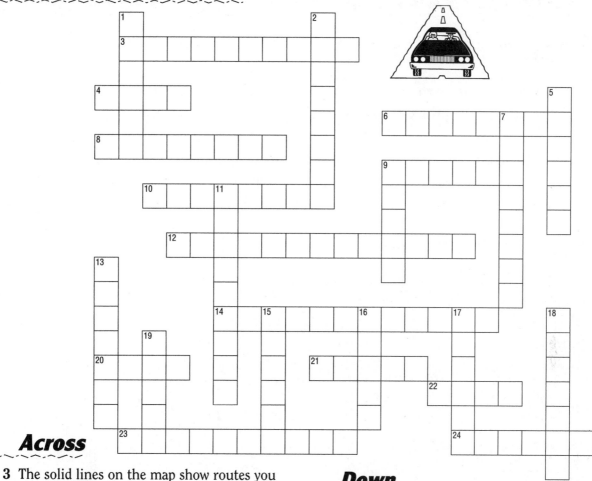

Across

3 The solid lines on the map show routes you can travel by _____.

4 You will pass through the town of _____ if you drive to Eagle from Denver.

6 Interstate 70 follows the path of the _____ River.

8 The air routes on this map are not curved, but _____.

9 Automobiles are _____ than airplanes.

10 To go from Denver to Glenwood Springs, you can travel on a highway or _____.

12 The most western city on this map served by airplanes is _____.

14 Route 82 passes through a high point in the Rocky Mountains at _____ Pass.

20 Interstate 70 runs from east to _____.

21 How many different kinds of transportation routes start in Denver?

22 Airplanes fly right _____ the high mountains.

23 Route 70 is an _____ highway, which means it goes across different states.

24 From this city, you can travel by rail, air, or car.

Down

1 Driving from Aspen to Glenwood Springs, you pass through this town.

2 The most western stop of the railroad is _____ Springs.

5 Air routes on this map are shown by a _____ line.

7 The fastest way to travel is by _____.

9 Colorado Springs is in which direction from Denver.

11 The only way you can get to _____ is by driving on Route 24.

13 U.S. 24 is the name of a _____.

15 Airplanes offer the most _____ route from Denver to Aspen.

16 The rail route to Glenwood Springs is farther in which direction than the highway route.

17 The routes of roads and railroads on this map are more _____ than the air routes.

18 If you drive northwest from Denver, you will soon reach _____.

19 You can get to this town either by car or by airplane.

Rain Forest
South America

Maps can be used to show how the environment changes over time. This map shows the decreasing size of the tropical rain forest in South America, because trees are cut for lumber and to make way for farms and roads. Scientists can use these maps to predict how changes in the rain forest will impact other parts of the environment, from the flow of the Amazon River to the climate of the entire world.

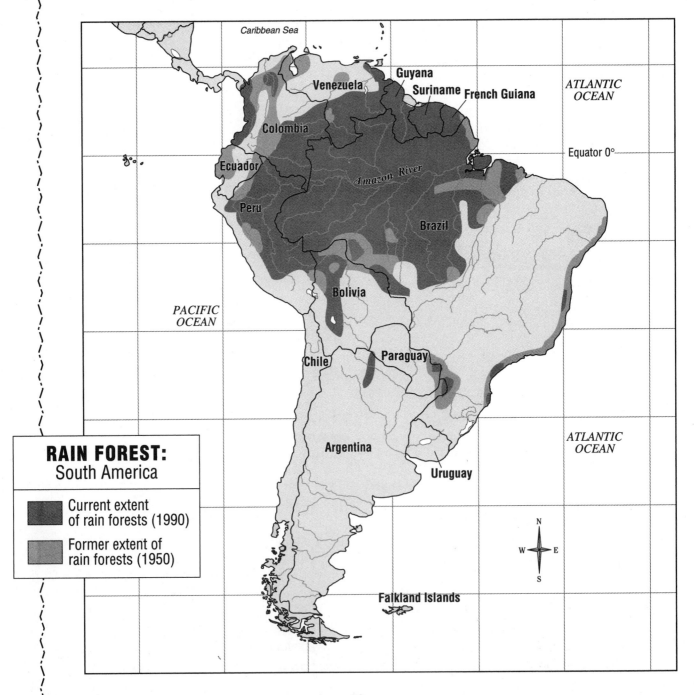

RAIN FOREST:
South America

- Current extent of rain forests (1990)
- Former extent of rain forests (1950)

Rain Forest

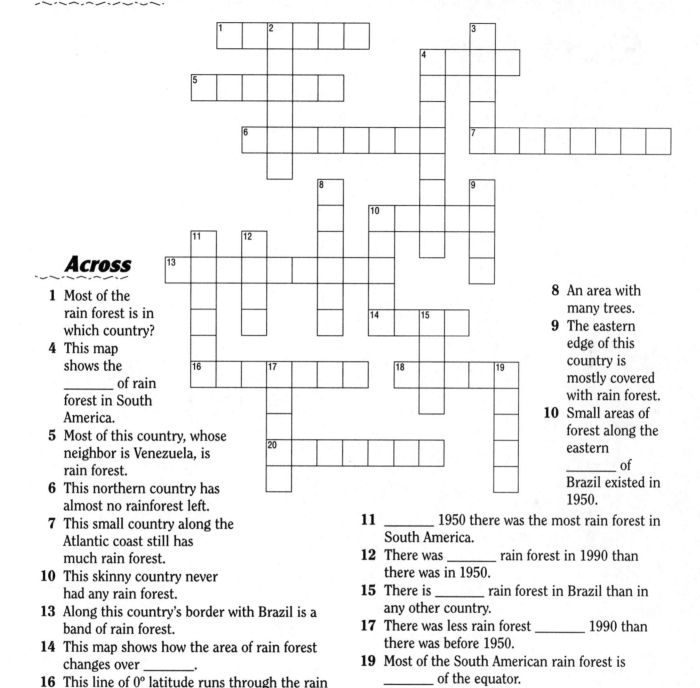

Across

1 Most of the rain forest is in which country?

4 This map shows the _____ of rain forest in South America.

5 Most of this country, whose neighbor is Venezuela, is rain forest.

6 This northern country has almost no rainforest left.

7 This small country along the Atlantic coast still has much rain forest.

10 This skinny country never had any rain forest.

13 Along this country's border with Brazil is a band of rain forest.

14 This map shows how the area of rain forest changes over _____.

16 This line of 0° latitude runs through the rain forest.

18 A forest is not a forest without _____.

20 This small country has lost most of its rain forest.

Down

2 Much of the rain forest is found along the _____ River.

3 This map shows the change of South American rain forest over 40 _____.

4 There is rain forest found along which ocean?

8 An area with many trees.

9 The eastern edge of this country is mostly covered with rain forest.

10 Small areas of forest along the eastern _____ of Brazil existed in 1950.

11 _____ 1950 there was the most rain forest in South America.

12 There was _____ rain forest in 1990 than there was in 1950.

15 There is _____ rain forest in Brazil than in any other country.

17 There was less rain forest _____ 1990 than there was before 1950.

19 Most of the South American rain forest is _____ of the equator.

DID YOU KNOW?

The term *rain forest* is used to describe a forest that receives more that 70 inches (1.8 m) of rain in a year. (Chicago, by comparison, receives only 35 inches per year.) Although rain forests cover only 6% of the earth's land, they are home to about three-quarters of all kinds of plants and animals.

Longitude and Latitude

South Asia

No matter where you are on earth, you can find out your location by using a special system called the global grid. This grid is made up of imaginary lines called latitude and longitude. If you imagine that the earth is an apple, lines of latitude, also called parallels, would slice the apple across into disks. The line around the middle is called the equator, and everything above that line is north; everything below it is south. Lines of longitude, also called meridians, would slice the apple from top to bottom into wedges. These lines meet at the top of the earth at the North Pole and at the bottom at the South Pole. A line that runs from north to south through England is called the Prime Meridian. All lines to the right of this are east; all lines to the left are west.

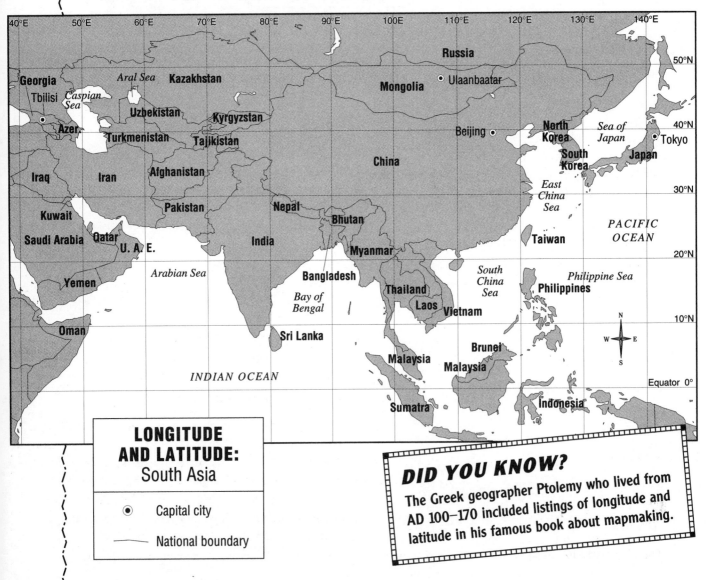

LONGITUDE AND LATITUDE:
South Asia

⊙ Capital city

—— National boundary

DID YOU KNOW?

The Greek geographer Ptolemy who lived from AD 100–170 included listings of longitude and latitude in his famous book about mapmaking.

Longitude and Latitude

Across

4 The line 10ºN crosses over the following countries: Phillipines, Vietnam, Thailand, and _____.

6 The _____ Sea is located where the lines 20ºN and 70ºE cross.

7 When listing the location of a place, the degree of latitude is always listed _____.

9 The line that is 0º latitude is also called the _____.

10 As you move north or south from the equator, lines of longitude become _____ to one another.

11 This tiny country, located on the 90º E meridian, is squeezed between China and India.

13 The capital of Mongolia is located at 48ºN, 108ºE.

18 The countries shown on this map make up the continent of _____.

20 The capital of Georgia, located at about 42ºN is called _____.

21 Longitude and latitude are measured in _____.

22 This large country spreads across Asia from 80ºE to 130ºE.

23 Lines of longitude, or meridians, run from north to _____.

24 The lines 50ºN and 100ºE cross in this country.

Down

1 Another word for lines of latitude is _____.

2 Between Japan and Korea, at 40ºN is the Sea of _____.

3 Lines that run across the globe east to west are called lines of _____.

5 Above the equator, the higher the number of latitude, the farther _____ you are.

8 Lines of latitude run from east to _____.

10 This large sea is actually a lake, and is located at 40ºN, 50ºE.

12 As you move closer to the equator, the temperature is usually _____.

14 When listing the location of a place, the degree of longitude is always listed _____.

15 The capital of China which is located on the 40th parallel is _____.

16 China is located in which direction from the Prime Meridian?

17 There are _____ degrees between the lines of latitude shown on this map.

19 Spell backwards this large country, which is located mostly above 50º N.

20 This capital city is located very close to the meridian 140ºE.

Elevation

Western United States

Elevation maps show how high a place is above sea level. For example, a mountain would have a higher elevation than a valley. Elevation is measured in feet or meters. This elevation map shows some of the highest areas of North America, the Rocky Mountains.

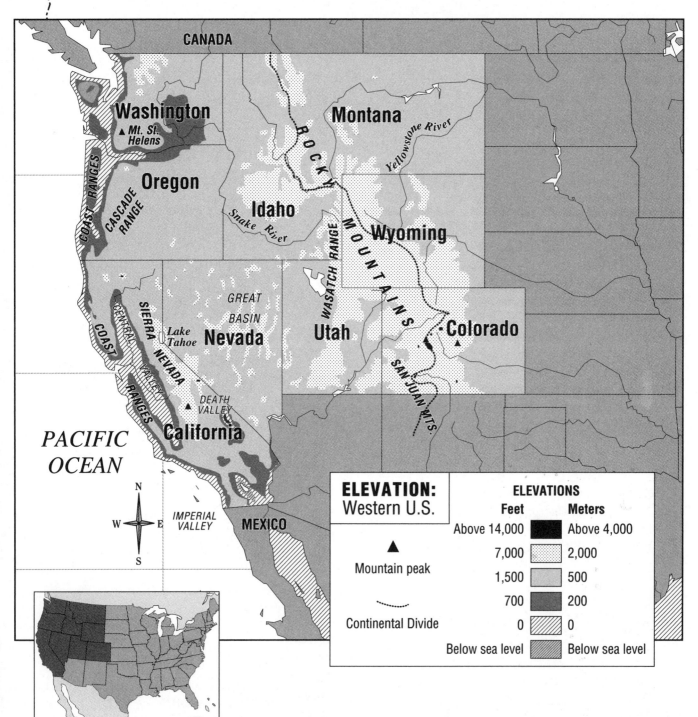

ELEVATION:
Western U.S.

▲

Mountain peak

······
Continental Divide

ELEVATIONS

	Feet		Meters
Above 14,000			Above 4,000
7,000			2,000
1,500			500
700			200
0			0
Below sea level			Below sea level

Elevation

Across

3 The elevation of California's Central Valley is _____ than most of the state.

5 An imaginary line called the Continental _____ runs along the Rocky Mountains.

9 The highest elevations are found among which landforms?

10 The Sierra Nevada Mountains are _____ than the Coast Ranges.

12 Elevation can be measured in feet or in _____.

14 The Sierra Nevada Mountains are the highest mountains in which state?

18 More than half of this state is covered with land above 7,000 feet.

20 Another word for a mountain.

21 Most of the Rocky Mountains are _____ 7,000 feet.

22 The western part of this state is mostly above 7,000 feet.

25 This state is home to the explosive Mt. St. Helens.

Down

1 The highest mountains on this map are above 14,000 _____.

2 On this state's border with California is the mountain lake called Lake Tahoe.

4 Most of this state is above 1,500 feet.

6 A group of mountains.

7 The climate is _____ at higher elevations.

8 These bodies of water flow from higher elevations to lower elevations.

11 The Snake River runs through this state on its way to Oregon.

12 This state's name makes it sound like it has a lot of mountains.

13 The Imperial _____ in California has very low elevation.

15 The biggest mountain range in the West is the _____ Mountains.

16 Along the Pacific _____, the elevation is very low.

17 Rivers carry rainwater _____ the mountains to the Pacific Ocean.

19 Death Valley in California is _____ sea level.

23 The Rocky Mountains range from south to _____.

24 In this state is the Wasatch Range.

DID YOU KNOW?

The Continental Divide is an imaginary line that runs along the spine of the Rocky Mountains. This line divides the areas where water drains into the Atlantic Ocean from those that drain into the Pacific Ocean. Rain drops that fall on opposite sides of this line eventually end up thousands of miles away from each other.

Name _____

Population Cartogram
World

The special kind of map on this page is called a *cartogram*. It is a map of the world, but something looks very different about it! Countries are the wrong size and shape. That's because a cartogram is not a picture of the world's geography. Instead it is a way to present information about the world. This cartogram shows the number of people, or population, of the world. The bigger a country appears on this map, the bigger is its population.

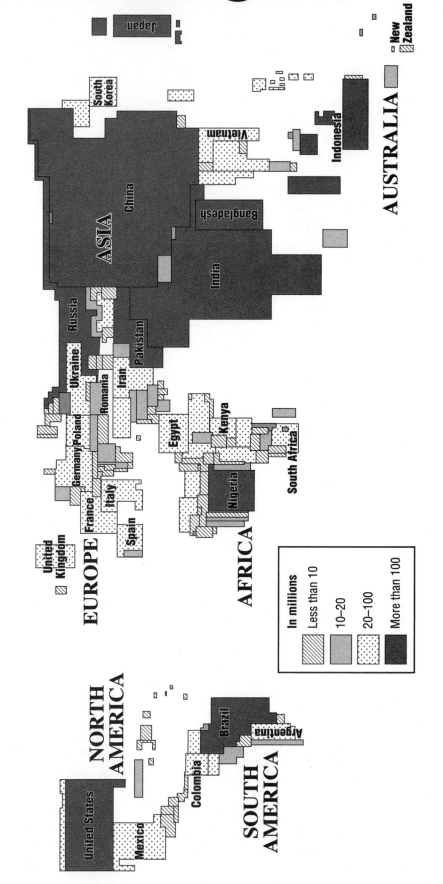

In millions
Less than 10
10–20
20–100
More than 100

Japan

New Zealand

South Korea

Vietnam

Indonesia

AUSTRALIA

China

ASIA

Bangladesh

India

Russia

Pakistan

Ukraine

Iran

Romania

Germany Poland

Egypt

Kenya

United Kingdom

France

Italy

Spain

EUROPE

Nigeria

South Africa

AFRICA

NORTH AMERICA

Brazil

Argentina

United States

Mexico

Colombia

SOUTH AMERICA

Population Cartogram

Across

4 This continent has one country with more than 100 million people.

6 This country, which is a group of islands near Australia, has more than 100 million people.

8 Where there are more people, there is a need for more _____.

10 This country has the most people in both North and South America.

11 Part of Russia is located on the continent of _____.

13 Brazil has the most people in this continent.

18 This country has the biggest population in Africa.

19 The smallest countries on this map have _____ than 10 million people.

20 The larger a country appears on this map, the _____ people it has.

21 This small island country has many people, more than 100 million!

Down

1 This country has the biggest population of South America.

2 This neighbor to the north of the United States has 20-100 million people.

3 Each year the population of the world _____.

5 Population is the measure of _____ who live in a place.

7 This continent has the most people.

9 A word for the number of people who live somewhere.

12 South of the United States is this country with between 20 and 100 million people.

13 The population of Vietnam is _____ than China.

14 This island continent has between 10 and 20 million people.

15 This country has the largest population in the world.

16 _____ of the countries in South America has more than 100 million people.

17 On this map a country with more people appears _____.

DID YOU KNOW?

The world population now is about 5.6 billion people. The United States has the third largest population, after China and India. Many experts expect that the world population will stabilize by the end of the next century.

Oceans
World

Although oceans cover nearly three-quarters of the earth's surface, most maps focus on land areas. Maps of oceans, however, can show many different things: from where certain fishes live to where the water is warmest. The map below shows ocean depths and major currents.

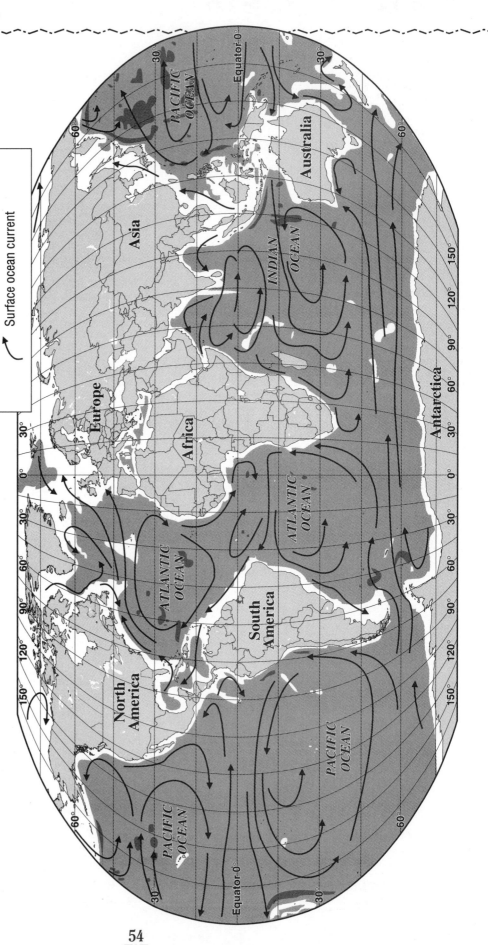

OCEANS: World

Depth		
Meters		**Feet**
0 to 200		0 to 600
200 to 6,000		600 to 18,000
More than 6,000		More than 18,000

↝ Surface ocean current

Oceans

Across

1 This continent is bordered by every ocean except the Atlantic.

4 One current flows up from Antarctica to this island continent.

7 Ocean depth is measured in meters or _____.

9 The ocean is more shallow _____ to land.

12 This imaginary line divides the globe into north and south.

13 A current runs west to east along this icy continent.

18 Is it true or false that a current in the South Atlantic flows counterclockwise?

19 This map might help you figure out where certain types of _____ live.

21 Are there deeper areas of ocean in the east side or west side of the Pacific?

22 A current along the California coast flows in which direction?

23 Off the east coast of Japan is an area where the ocean is _____ than 18,000 feet deep.

Down

1 This ocean lies between the Americas and Africa.

2 This is the biggest ocean.

3 One current flows across the Atlantic from North America to _____.

5 A current flows west along the southern coast of _____, the biggest state of the United States.

6 The oceans are usually _____ away from the land.

8 This map shows the depth of all of the _____.

10 This map would be useful if you were traveling by _____.

11 If you were traveling by sailboat, what other information might be helpful?

12 A current across the North Atlantic flows from west to _____.

14 A current right off the east Asian coast flows in which direction?

15 A current flows south between the island of Madagascar and this continent.

16 Do the currents around Hawaii flow clockwise or counterclockwise?

17 The deepest ocean areas on this map are more than 6,000 _____.

20 This ocean lies between Asia, Africa, and Australia.

DID YOU KNOW?

The deepest point in the ocean is the Marianas Trench in the Pacific Ocean, which is 36,163 feet (11,022 m) below the surface. If Mt. Everest, the world's highest mountain, were turned upside down and placed in the Marianas Trench, there would be more than a mile of extra room.

Answers

Highways
Arizona
page 7

Temperature
Florida
page 9

Vegetation
World
page 11

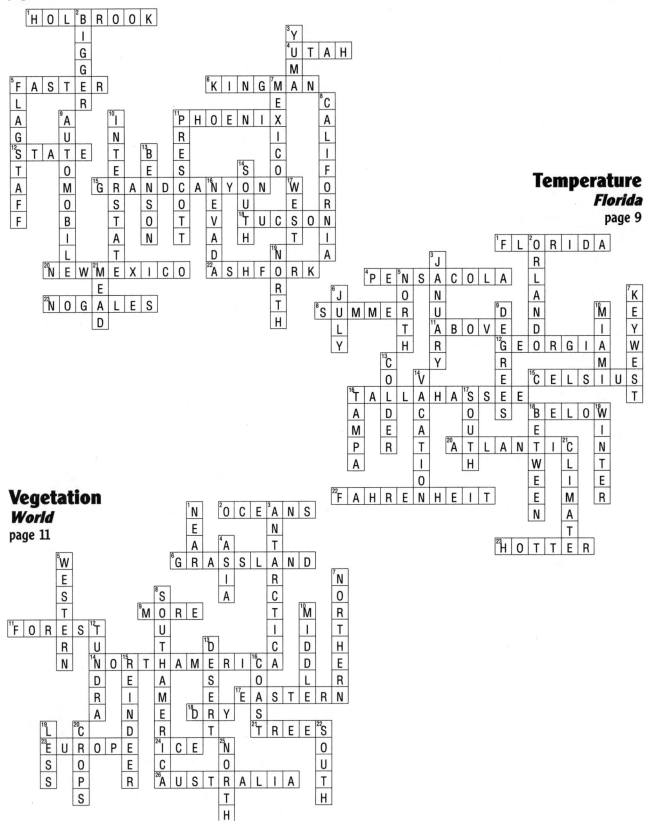

Growth of Railroads
Europe
page 13

Land Use
Colorado
page 15

Products
Montana
page 17

Precipitation
Africa
page 19

City Map
London
page 21

Indian Culture Areas
North America
page 23

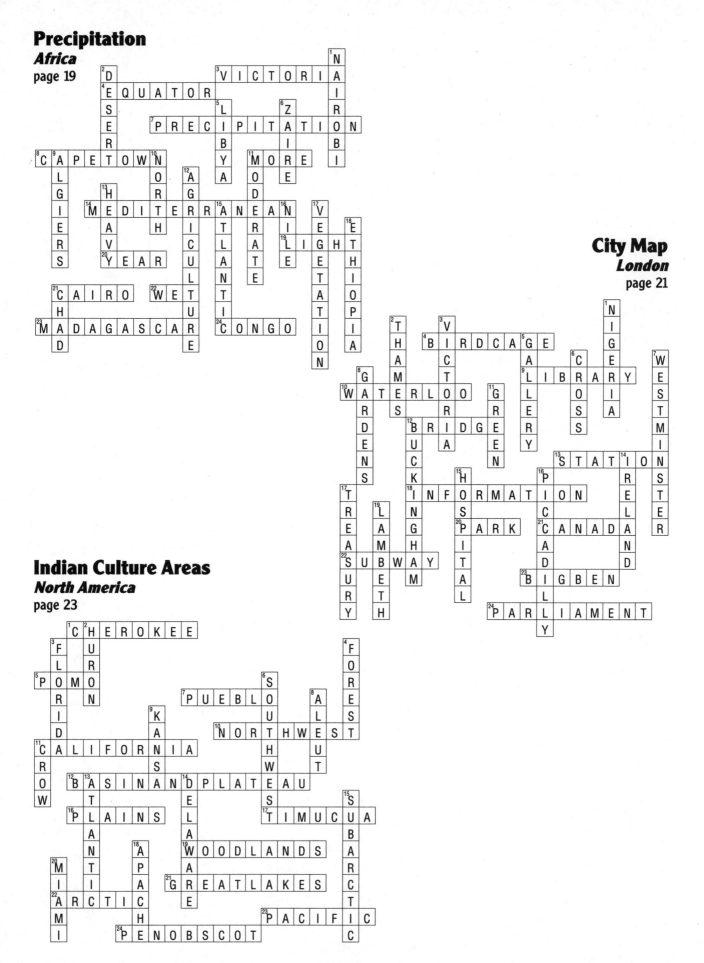

Climate
Europe
page 25

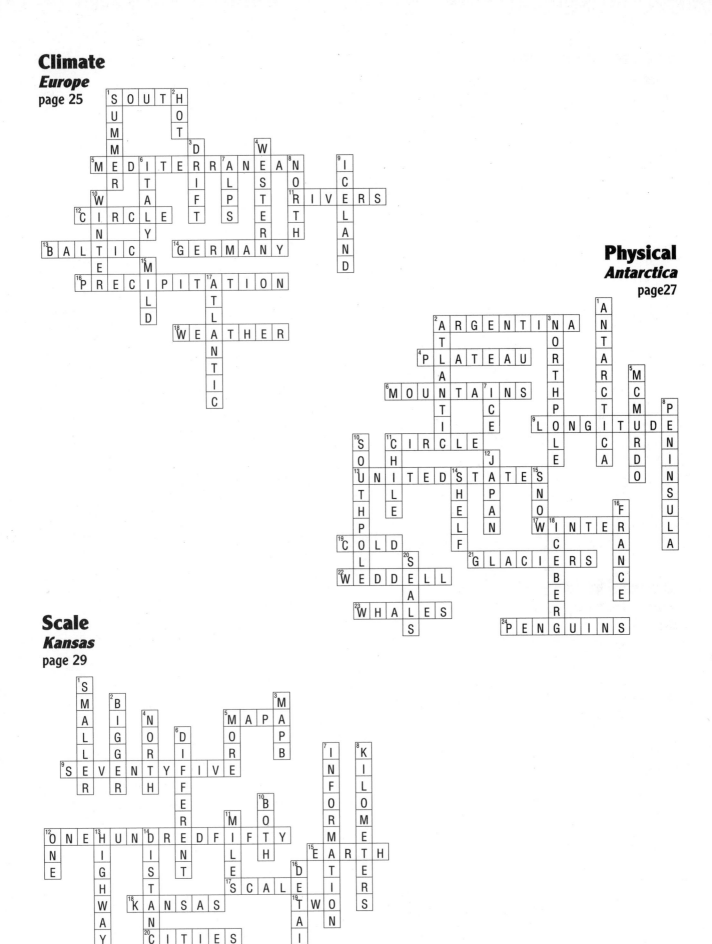

Physical
Antarctica
page27

Scale
Kansas
page 29

Endangered Species
Africa
page 31

Religions
World
page 33

Comparing Maps
Baseball Teams, 1952–1995
page 35

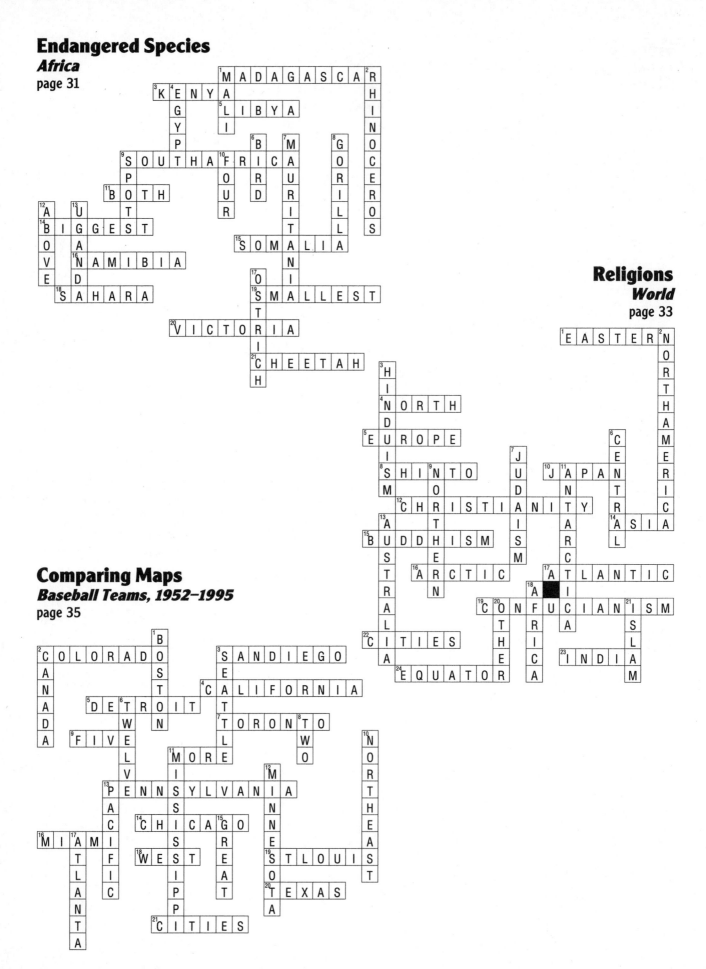

Subway
Washington, D.C., Metro
page 37

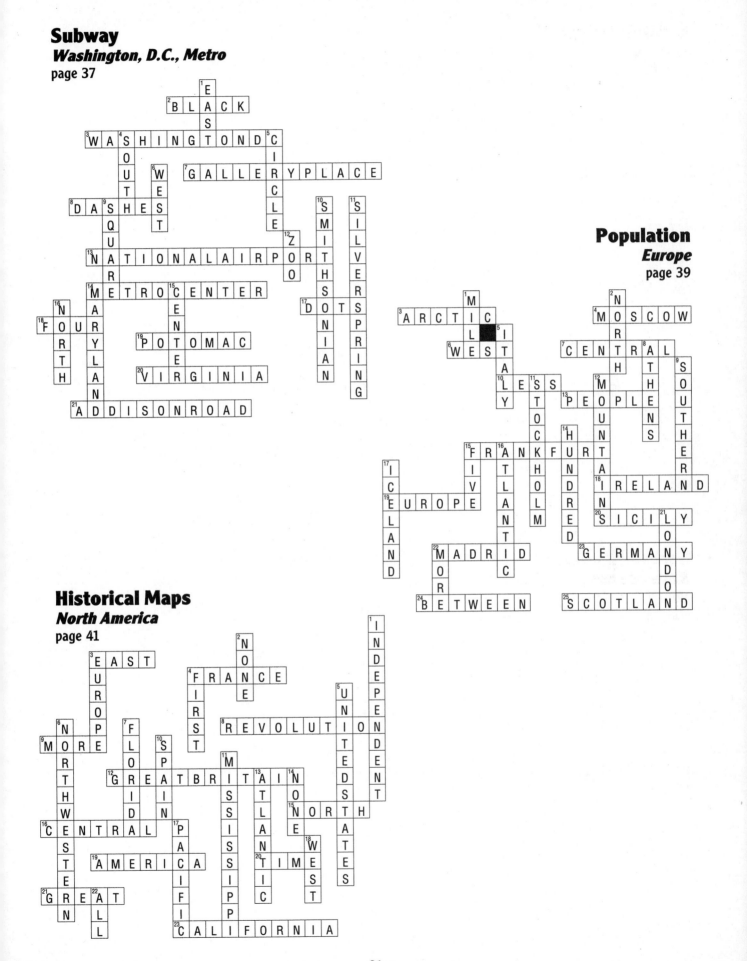

Population
Europe
page 39

Historical Maps
North America
page 41

Natural Hazards
Australia
page 43

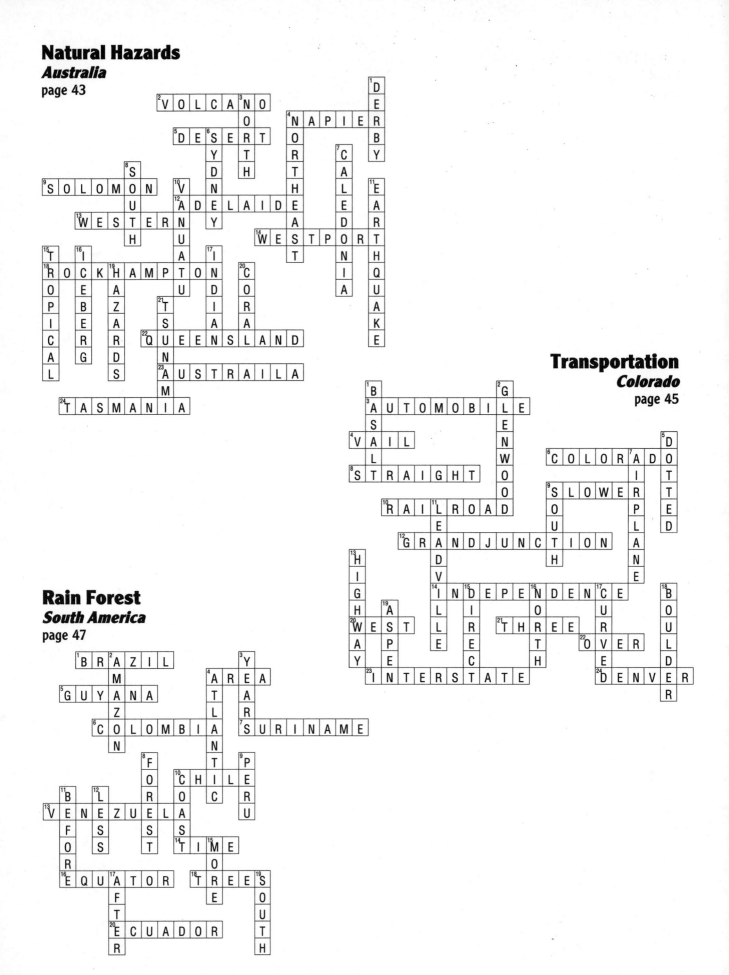

Transportation
Colorado
page 45

Rain Forest
South America
page 47

Longitude and Latitude
South Asia
page 49

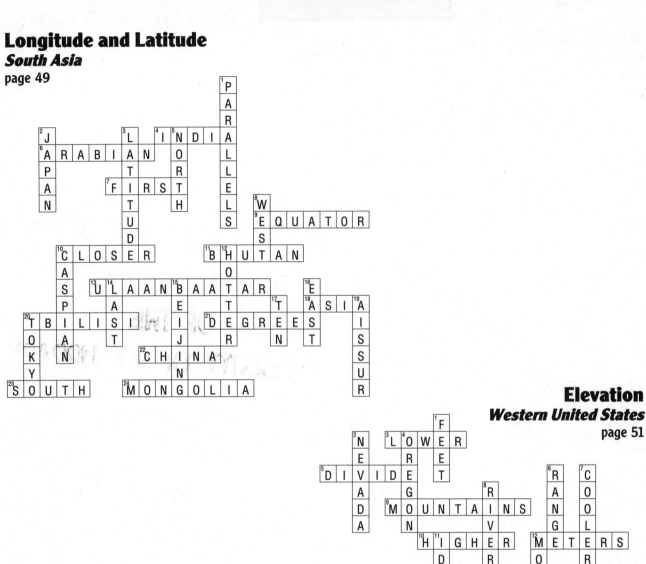

Population Cartogram
World
page 53

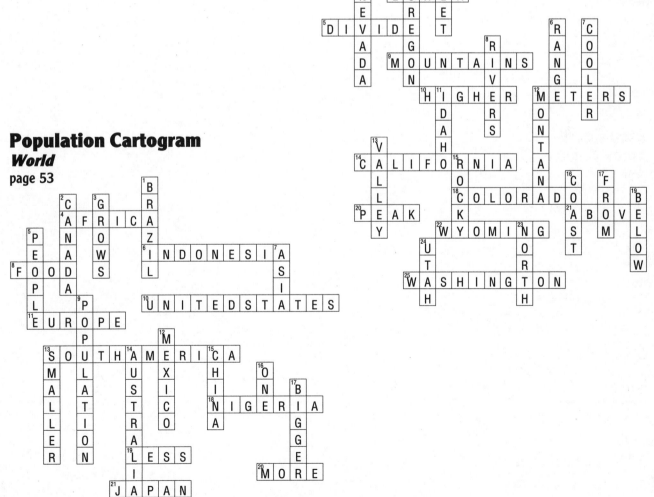

Elevation
Western United States
page 51

Oceans
World
page 55